Making Leaf Rubbings

MAKING

Leaf

Rubbings

by Mary Lou Burch

drawings by Becky Anderson

The Stephen Greene Press
Brattleboro, Vermont

This book has been produced in the United States of America. It is designed by R. L. Dothard Associates, and published by the Stephen Greene Press, Brattleboro, Vermont 05301

LIBRARY OF CONGRESS CATALOGING IN PUBLICATION DATA

Burch, Mary Lou, 1914-
    Making leaf rubbings.

    Bibliography: p.
    Includes index.
    1. Rubbing. 2. Leaves. 3. Leaf prints. I. Title.
II. Title: Leaf rubbings.
TT912.B87   760   78-58678
ISBN 0-8289-0334-4

CONTENTS

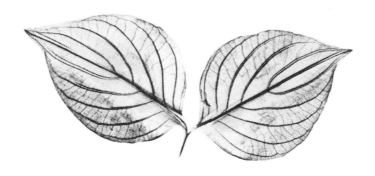

THE MANY PLEASURES
OF LEAF RUBBING

MAKING LEAF RUBBINGS is fun for everyone in the family, from pre-schooler to senior citizen. Some members will have only a few minutes to spend while others will become absorbed for hours. Leaf rubbing fits either situation because there is no elaborate preparation or cleanup involved.

In addition to the fun of making the rubbings, there are many other pleasures waiting for you as you pursue this hobby. You can enjoy the colors, the fragrances, and the textures of the leaves as you pick them and work with them. You can appreciate the shapes of individual plants and the effect of combining them with other plants to form a landscape. Searching for designs will sharpen your awareness of the beauty and the immense variety of natural forms. Your life will be enriched by time spent outdoors, learning from and learning about the natural world.

HOW TO MAKE A LEAF RUBBING

The Basic Process

Making a leaf rubbing is very simple:

1. *You will notice that one side of the leaf is smooth while the other (the underside) has ribs and veins more exposed. Lay the leaf you want to rub so that the underside is up. Be sure to place the leaf on a hard, smooth surface.*

2. *Cover the leaf with paper.*

3. *Locate the covered leaf by rubbing your fingers over the paper.*

4. *Hold the leaf firmly in place with your*

left hand (if you are right handed) by pressing on it through the paper with your fingers.

5. With your right hand, move the rubbing crayon firmly across the paper where it covers the leaf. Use short strokes. Press hard enough so that the raised ribs, veins, and edges are darker than the rest of the leaf.

6. To complete the rubbing, carefully shift your fingers to a section already finished, taking great care not to move the paper or the leaf as you do so.

You may have to practice a little before you produce rubbings that satisfy you. The pages immediately following will tell you what kind of paper and rubbing crayon to use and will suggest ways to improve your technique.

4   HOW TO MAKE A RUBBING

The Paper

You can make a visible rubbing on almost any kind of paper, even a grocery bag. However, to get a rubbing that has interesting detail you will need a smooth, lightweight paper. Inexpensive typing paper will give good results. Newsprint will give fair results, but it is a little too rough and textured to be ideal. The more expensive linen weaves and other textured papers are not as good because they distort the rubbings slightly.

One of the most satisfactory kinds of paper for beginners is a roll of white shelf paper. Avoid the plastic-coated and very heavy kinds. One advantage to a roll of paper is that you can rub larger leaves and ferns that wouldn't fit on smaller sized paper. Also, it is convenient to be able to unroll the paper and start over if you don't like what you're doing; you feel more free to experiment.

Art supply shops carry elegant, fine papers suitable for your most artistic projects, but it is a good idea to experiment first with less ex-

pensive paper. Since the wax of the rubbing crayon is usually going to cover the paper, the rubbings made on shelf paper are sometimes just as effective as those made on fine papers. You can also experiment with scraps of colored paper, trying out various colors of rubbing crayons. Colored paper bags from shops or colored art tissue are worth trying.

Rubbing Crayons

Many children are introduced to leaf rubbing in school art or nature classes using ordinary school crayons. While the outline of the leaf shows up plainly, the finer details of interior veins are blurred and uninteresting. The soft wax and pointed ends of most ordinary crayons make them unsatisfactory for leaf rubbing. However, Prang Kantroll pressed crayons work quite well, if you use the blunt end. They are inexpensive, and come in a good assortment of colors.

The rubbing wax used for gravestone and brass rubbings is probably the best kind to use for leaf rubbings. This is available at many arts and crafts supply houses, or can be ordered from Oldstone Enterprises, 77 Summer Street, Boston, Mass. 02110. You can send for their brochure on rubbing supplies and make your selection. These may seem a little expensive, but even the smallest rubbing wedge will last for years.

Begin by using black or brown. The quality is better than most other colors. Later, after you've become expert, you may enjoy experimenting with various colors on different colors of paper. Sometimes you may want a special effect for a project and prefer rubbings with a softer appearance and less contrast.

Rubbing Techniques

Part of the fun in making leaf rubbings comes from developing your own techniques. Sometimes, short strokes all going one way produce the best results. On other leaves, a back-and-

forth motion seems to work better. Experience and experiment will help you determine which techniques work best for you, but there are a few simple rules you should keep in mind.

1. *Complete one small area of a leaf before moving to another.*

2. *Avoid using the point of the rubbing crayon; rub with the broad side. The size of the leaf will be a factor in your decision which surface of the crayon to use.*

3. *Keep your pressure on the crayon or wax as even as possible to avoid streaks in the rubbing.*

The most common problem for beginners is that of keeping the leaf or the paper from slipping. To avoid this, press your fingers on one edge of the leaf while you mark out the stalk and the midrib with a good strong stroke. Then hold the midrib at the center while you rub the top half of the leaf. Gradually move your fingers down the midrib, holding firmly as you rub each section. Don't go back over a

part that is already finished because the leaf
will slip slightly and you'll get a double line.
The size and shape of the leaf will often be a
factor in deciding how to hold it. If one way
doesn't work for you, try another.

Another common problem has to do with
the surface on which the leaf is placed. Sometimes a surface such as a wooden table looks
perfectly smooth, but your rubbing will reflect
the wood grain. Glass, metal, or plastic surfaces such as Formica make excellent back-
grounds. If nothing better is available, you can

use a magazine. It won't be quite as good as a harder surface, but it is usually available.

The Leaves

In looking for leaves to rub, don't assume that they have to be big and tough. Sometimes

even very fragile-looking ferns and delicate wildflowers make excellent rubbings. Anything with a raised surface is worth trying, but you will soon discover that some leaves are much better than others.

The number of times you can use the same leaf for rubbing will vary greatly, depending on the species and also on the time of year. In the spring when many leaves are tender and juicy, they may deteriorate quickly. Pick several leaves of each kind you plan to rub. You might want to take a magazine with you and place your leaves carefully between the pages. That way they'll be sure to arrive home in good condition.

Some of the enjoyment of making leaf rubbings comes from the search for different leaves to rub—leaves of trees, shrubs, flowering plants, wildflowers, ferns, groundcovers, weeds, and grasses. The variety is almost endless. Even garden vegetables have leaves that are interesting to rub.

You don't need a garden or a forest to supply your leaves, either. Weeds growing in the

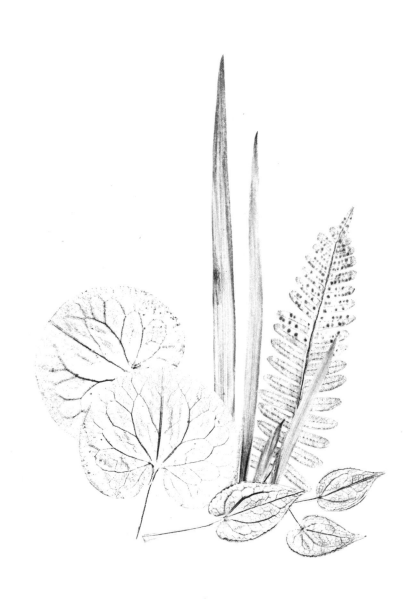

cracks of a city sidewalk, or along the railroad tracks, or by a parking lot will provide plenty of interesting material. Sometimes the best rubbings come from the least impressive plants. A vacant lot will amaze you with the variety of leaves it provides.

Some leaves make the best rubbings if they are used as soon as you pick them, but for many others it is better to dry them a day or two before making the rubbing. To dry them, simply place them carefully between the pages of a book or magazine, preferably one that doesn't have glossy paper.

The Finished Rubbing

It is usually not practical to try to stay within the boundaries of the leaf when making a rubbing. It is much easier to cut away the background and mount the finished rubbing on a clean sheet of paper. All of the illustrated rubbings up to this point have been handled in this way. However, there are several other possibilities.

Often the background shading adds to the attractiveness of the rubbing. If you plan to leave the background, color it all uniformly, using very even pressure to avoid streaks.

Another possibility is to rub carefully, trying to stay within the edges of the leaf as much as possible. This is much easier to do if you are rubbing something like lilac or dogwood leaves, which have no lobes or teeth.

Even with care, you will probably have a few marks outside the edge of the leaf. Sometimes you can achieve an attractive "frame" for your rubbing by adding a few more judiciously placed marks.

The character of the material being rubbed will help you decide whether or not to cut out your rubbing. For obvious reasons you are not going to want to undertake anything as tedious as cutting away the background from some of the lacy ferns or from a composition of flowering grasses.

ORGANIZING A COLLECTION

NEARLY EVERYONE enjoys making a collection, especially if there is the challenge to continue to improve or complete it. A collection of rubbings can be organized in a scrapbook, a photo album, or portfolio. Another very good way to keep a collection in order is to make a scroll out of a roll of shelf paper, rolling up your work as you complete it.

Collections can be simple or technical. Small children like to see how many different kinds of leaves they can find to rub. The dif-

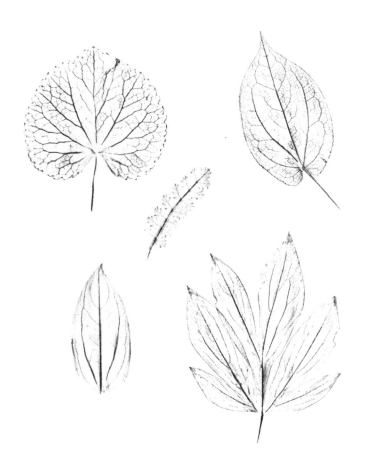

ferences may be in size, in shape, or in pattern of veins. A collection showing a leaf from each different tree in one's own yard, school grounds, or the immediate neighborhood is

one good project. A visit to a park or an arboretum furnishes additional material.

It is not necessary to attach any educational significance to leaf rubbing, but a great deal of learning will take place as a by-product of the craft. For instance, skill in classifying is developed when leaves are separated according to shape, size, and venation. Further, this classifying improves visual perception, the development of which is an important objective in current educational thinking. The fact that making rubbings exposes leaf characteristics very gradually means that it is a particularly good means of developing ability in perceiving likenesses and differences.

Tree leaves are not the only possibility for collections. If you are interested in wild flowers, rub a leaf from each variety you find. If you have a flower garden, make a collection of rubbings of the leaves you find there. Appreciating the foliage will add to your enjoyment of the flowers.

You will discover that leaves of some plants can be rubbed only in the spring because the foliage disappears during the summer; others remain green until frost, while still others are evergreen. The remarkable variations in leaf texture, from soft and woolly to tough and leathery, will affect the quality of the rubbings. When you rub some leaves, they will collapse under the pressure of the rubbing

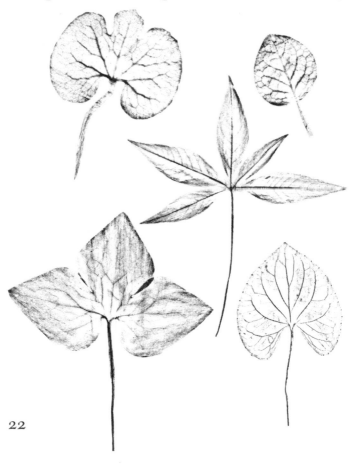

wax. Sometimes this leaves a green impression of the leaf on the back of the rubbing.

Without making any specific effort to do so, you will soon learn to identify plants by their foliage instead of by their blossoms. This knowledge is useful if you want to move these plants when they are not in bloom.

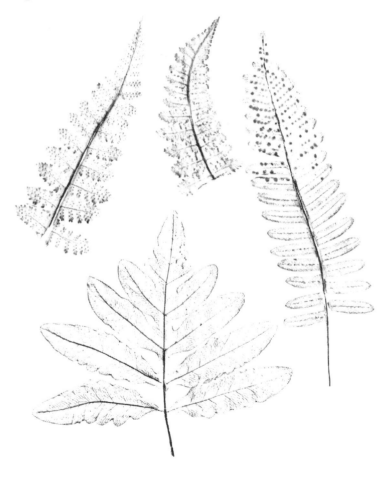

Tree Identification

The most obvious learning experience to come from leaf rubbing is that of tree identification. From the observation of the differences in shapes of leaves it is a short step to the observation of the details useful in pinning down the species of tree that the leaves came from. Whether you are interested in learning more about trees and other plants for yourself or are looking for a method of introducing children to the fascinating subject of identification, you will find leaf rubbings are helpful. Learning to identify trees is something like a detective game. Through rubbing individual leaves you will learn many of the clues to look for.

A prominent feature of some leaves is the *lobe* (see top of opposite page). The indentation between two lobes is called the *sinus*. The number of lobes on a leaf and the depth of the sinus are two clues you can use to help identify the tree.

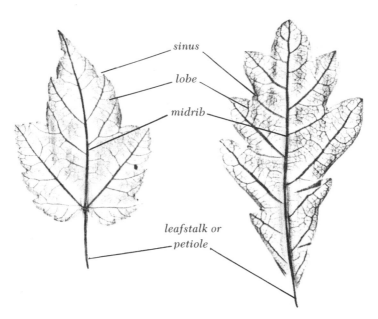

sinus

lobe

midrib

leafstalk or
petiole

Another important matter to consider in plant identification is the edge of the leaf. Below are several frequently seen types of leaf edge or margin.

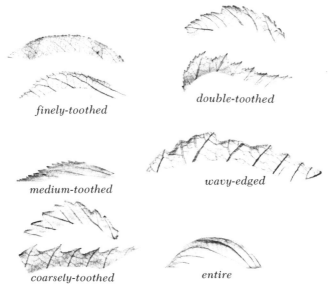

finely-toothed

double-toothed

medium-toothed

wavy-edged

coarsely-toothed

entire

The arrangement of leaves on the twig is also an identifying characteristic of tree species. In the rubbing on the left below, the leaf arrangement is *opposite*; at right, leaves grow from the stem in the order called *alternate*.

Ferns, Grasses and Weeds

Ferns are another good subject for a collection. Those who have never studied these plants will be surprised to find how many different kinds there are and how different each kind is from the others. A collection of grass

rubbings also leads to many surprises. Even
the vegetable garden provides leaves for an
elegant collection of rubbings.

One of the most surprising collections you
can rub is that of weeds. The beauty of their
leaves usually lies unnoticed, but very often
they make rubbings that are as exotic as rub-

bings of the most prized plants. After making a rubbing of a dandelion leaf, show it to your friends to see if they can identify this "rare" plant. Few people fail to exclaim about the beauty of this artistic rubbing; fewer still can identify it from the rubbing.

Evergreens

Many people have the mistaken idea that winter brings an end to leaf rubbing. While the choice of materials may not be as wide as it

is during the summer, there are still a surprising number of leaves that are evergreen or
semi-evergreen. The leaves of many of the
broad-leaved evergreens such as rhododen-
dron, laurel, and pieris make better rubbings
if the leaves are dried under a heavy book for a
few days.

The needled evergreens are a conspicuous
element of the winter landscape, and of the

evergreens the pine is probably the most familiar. In fact, some people call all needled evergreens pine, indicating that they have never noticed the distinct differences among evergreens. Make some rubbings and you'll see how easy it is to identify them.

Even without a book you will recognize the pines by their long needles bundled together in groups of two, three, or five, depending on which kind of pine they're from. You'll find that similar clues to the identity of the other needled evergreens will show up in rubbings. With the help of a field guide, you'll have no trouble identifying and remembering them.

Not all of the needled evergreens lend themselves to rubbing. Spruce, for example, has needles that are sharp and stiff and grow in spirals around the twigs, making rubbing practically impossible. Other evergreens can be rubbed more successfully if you remove about half of the needles, so boughs lie flat. This will enable you to avoid the muddy look of too many overlapping needles in the rubbing.

USING YOUR RUBBINGS

AFTER A LITTLE PRACTICE, you will be making beautiful rubbings. At this point, your thoughts will turn to ways of getting greater enjoyment from them by using them or displaying them in some way. Your first idea will probably be to make a picture or a wall hanging. If your first attempts don't please you, don't be discouraged. It takes time to get things just right.

Wall Hangings

One way to make a wall hanging is to arrange several cutout rubbings within a frame. You

will probably reject many of your rubbings because they are too subtle and delicate to be effective at any distance. After you have made your selection, keep trying different combinations until you find a composition that is pleasing. Finally, try different ways of enhancing the effect by using a colored background, matting, or frame. You may end up preferring a simple white background with a narrow black frame, but you'll enjoy experimenting. You might also like to experiment with colored rubbing wax. A watercolor wash is another possibility.

Instead of cutting out your rubbings to compose your picture, it is sometimes better to arrange your composition first, especially if you are rubbing grasses. This is an interesting exercise in balance and proportion since you can add, subtract, or reposition parts of the material. Usually the effect is improved with a little judicious pruning to avoid too much overlapping. When you are satisfied with your arrangement, place the paper over it and make your rubbing.

Other Ways to Display Rubbings

There are many ways to display rubbings in informal rooms such as playrooms or children's rooms. Instead of framing them, simply paste them to a large piece of posterboard. Be sure to move the rubbings around until you find a pleasing relationship before applying paste.

Sometimes, the shelf paper you've been making your rubbings on can be unrolled and hung horizontally around the room, or vertically from ceiling to floor, depending on which direction you've made the rubbings. If you do this, you'll probably get better results if you cut off part of the shelf paper to experiment with first, repeating only your successes on the section you use for display.

Exhibits on bulletin boards have the advantage of being easily changed. If you don't have a bulletin board, you can easily make one by stapling burlap over a large piece of cardboard cut from a packing box. An alternate display

background can easily be made by hemming the ends of a length of burlap or any other heavy fabric, inserting dowels in both hems and hanging it by a cord.

A clothesline tied between two points is a different kind of exhibit area. Children like to hang their art work with clip clothespins.

You will probably think of other ways to help children exhibit their rubbings, such as pinning them to draperies or curtains, or fastening them to windows. For the latter, fold a small piece of cellophane tape or masking tape so that it has a sticky surface front and back, one side for the leaf, the other for the glass.

Decorating Stationery

If you are using plain sheets for stationery, rubbing a small leaf in the corner adds interest and individuality. This works best if the paper is smooth and untextured. If you don't want to bother cutting out the rubbing and pasting it on the stationery, you'll need to be extra careful to keep the design looking neat. Try using a

very light stroke to bring out the outline of the leaf. Then, using very short strokes, rub within the outline. A few marks out of place are not objectionable and, after a little practice, you can do it very quickly.

Instead of always using a small leaf, you may sometimes want to use a tip of a branch with several small leaves, the tip of some flowering grass, or a single leaflet from a fern frond. Experiment on scratch paper until you find just what you want. A larger leaf could decorate the front of plain, folded notepaper, leaving the inside for the message.

LEAF RUBBING STATIONERY 39

Gifts for Children to Make

Children enjoy making small gifts using their leaf rubbings. They can make attractive book markers by mounting small rubbings on pieces of colored construction paper.

Another possible gift is a booklet showing their best rubbings. Older children could

write some facts about each leaf: what kind it is, where they found it, interesting things they may have learned about it.

Making gift wrapping is an interesting project. Explore various possibilities such as using colored rubbing crayon on various colors of paper. Try making rubbings on colored tissue paper. The art tissue you get in craft shops is quite strong and comes in good colors. Gift wrapping can be made either by rubbing the tissue and lining it with shelf paper or by making the rubbings on the shelf paper and covering it with tissue for extra elegance. Gift tags can be made from a folded piece of paper decorated with a rubbing of a small leaf.

Book covers can be made from shelf paper decorated with rubbings. For this project, a large fern or leaf is usually more effective than a miscellaneous collection of smaller leaves.

A Scrapbook

A scrap book of your favorite rubbings is a great conversation piece if left where guests are likely to pick it up and look through it. Keep a dried leaf, some paper, and a rubbing crayon nearby because guests usually ask how the rubbings were made and like to try out the process. You'll enjoy watching their pleasure as they discover the simple beauty of making leaf rubbings.

The preparation of such a scrapbook is

another opportunity for using your artistic judgment. Which leaves combine best to make an attractive page? Do you prefer a set, regular pattern, or would you rather create a design with random arrangement?

Cutout leaf rubbings are very effective against the black sheets of photo albums. If you buy one with plastic covers for each page, you won't have to paste the leaves and can change them whenever you feel like it.

If you decide to paste rubbings in your own book, be sure to use a good grade of nonstaining library paste. Rubber cement will discolor and show through the rubbings after a year or two.

Other Ways to Use Your Rubbings

There are many ways to use your rubbings to decorate the accessories in your home. Plain, untextured window shades, lampshades, or place mats all can be made more interesting with the addition of well-made rubbings.

Table mats to protect furniture from damp flower pots are attractive and easy to make. Begin with a piece of cardboard cut the size you want. Cover it with fabric or colored paper for a background. Arrange a design of leaf rubbings on this and cover it with a piece of glass cut to the size of the backing. Bind the edges with craft tape. You can use the same procedure to make coasters.

An inexpensive wastebasket can be transformed into a decorator's item. It is possible to cut a piece of shelf paper to go around the wastebasket and carefully make rubbings directly on the paper. However, you will probably get better results in less time if you cut out the rubbings and fasten them with nonstaining glue or paste to a previously covered or painted basket.

A set of matching desk accessories can be made using your choice rubbings. A sturdy box covered with paper and decorated with rubbings becomes an attractive letter holder. An orange-juice can becomes a pencil holder. You can buy wooden boxes at craft shops to make card files.

A coat or two of Krylon (a clear acrylic spray coating) makes a good protective finish for any painted item decorated with rubbings. Krylon can also be used on a paper background, but it increases the transparency of the paper so that any colored design or lettering will show through. You could paint the object before applying the paper, apply two coats of paper, or completely cover the background with the rubbings to avoid this problem. However, instead of using Krylon, it might be simpler to cover the rubbings with a sheet of clear plastic before finishing the edges with craft tape.

OTHER KINDS OF RUBBINGS

A NY RAISED or incised markings on a hard surface will yield a rubbing. Therefore the techniques of leaf rubbing can easily be adapted to produce handsome rubbings, through an activity that is pleasant and absorbing.

Bark Rubbings

Making bark rubbings is a good project for a pleasant winter day. As you choose tree trunks to rub, notice the subtle differences in color as they vary from white to silvery gray to reddish

brown to deep brown to black. Also note the variations in design from one species to another, and from young trees to mature trees of the same species.

Rubbings show off the designs and patterns of the bark in a dramatic way. The differences are so distinct that they are important in identifying trees, especially in winter. The bark of white birches is smooth, satiny, and easy to rub. The pattern has a definite horizontal direction. Mature maples and pines have deep furrows that produce interesting patterns of a completely different sort.

For bark rubbings, use a sheet of paper big enough so that the pattern repetition shows up. Some of the barks are so rough that you have to work carefully in order not to tear the paper. Fastening your paper to the trunk with masking tape will help keep it from slipping. Use the broadest side of the rubbing crayon and use only medium pressure until you get the hang of it. Don't quit if the first one you try doesn't come out. A little practice will lead to very satisfactory rubbings.

Making Rubbings Indoors

There are several ways to prepare your name or initials for rubbing.

1. *Write your name in script on heavy paper or lightweight cardboard. Cut out the name so that the width of the writing line is about an eighth of an inch thick.*

2. *Write your name by carefully squeezing glue out of a tube. Allow at least a day for it to dry before making the rubbing.*

3. *Print your name with a label-making machine.*

4. *Write or print your name on a smooth pine board or on heavy cardboard, going over it several times so that the letters are indented.*

5. *Carve your name or initials in a block of wood or a bar of soap.*

You can provide entertainment at a birthday party for children by preparing the names of the guests in one of the ways described. Place the names under blank place mats that you have cut out of shelf paper. Then have each child rub his place mat with the blunt end of a crayon until his name appears.

When the weather is really impossible, you can explore the relief and the indented surfaces around the house. Children enjoy the search for designs, which occur on all sorts of articles such as fancy dishes, decorative metal pieces, baskets, kitchen appliances, grillwork, bricks in a fireplace, and the bark of the log for the fire.

Point out to children that most man-made designs are based on something found in nature and suggest that they find examples to test

this fact. It is usually easy to see the relation-ship between a stylized design and the leaf, flower, shell, wave, or other natural source that inspired it.

You can add a different element to these activities by comparing the designs made by craftsmen of different countries. You can usu-ally determine where the article was made by looking on the back or the bottom. It may sur-prise you to find so many foreign places repre-sented by common items in your home.

Another way to provide entertainment for your young guests is to let them make rub-bings of old greeting cards. Save those that have a raised or indented design. Show them how to rub the design on some shelf paper with a rubbing crayon; they will keep busy for hours. You will be interested to note how much the design in the rubbing differs in effect from the brightly colored original.

Souvenirs

When you go on a vacation, be sure to pack your rubbing crayon and paper. Even on a short trip you're sure to find a tree, a shrub, or a weed that is different from those at home. If you travel to an area with a different climate, your appreciation of the differences in growing things will be sharpened if you are looking for new leaves to rub.

On a vacation at the seashore you will find some interesting things to experiment with. The curved surfaces of clam shells and sand dollars require patience and care, but they can be rubbed. The precision with which even the most common things in nature are designed is often an astonishing revelation.

Often, a spot of particular interest will be marked by a plaque that can be rubbed. Whether the legend commemorates an historic event or points out a special significance such as the tallest, longest, or biggest, you can take home a rubbing that will bring back memories of the day you were there.

Gravestone and Brass Rubbings

On some vacations you can make elegant rubbings of gravestones and brasses which you can carry home in a mailing tube for later framing. For a large, important rubbing of this sort, you probably will want to buy the special paper developed for this purpose. The rubbing techniques are the same as those used for leaf rubbing, except for a few details.

You will need to brush the stone or brass to be sure it is free of dirt before you begin. For a large rubbing, it is important to tape the paper in place so that there is no danger of its slipping while work is in progress. You will still be using short strokes, but since you want to make a dark rubbing, you will use a harder stroke and go over it several times to build up a solid surface of wax. Finish one small area before going on to the next and resist the temptation to go back over a section already finished.

Be sure to secure permission whenever you can to make rubbings in cemeteries. Caretakers, sextons, town officials, churchmen, historical society members, are the ones to ask. Too many cemeteries have been closed to the public because of the discourtesy of visitors, including gravestone rubbers.

Many people planning trips abroad set aside a day or two to make rubbings of memorial brasses in old churches and cathedrals. Even if your travels are limited to this country, you may still be able to make your own brass rubbings. When you are in any of the major cities, you can inquire if any of the art stores have replicas or smaller copies of some of the European brasses. For a small fee you can visit one of these stores and make your own rubbings. The result of rubbing a replica is indistinguishable from a rubbing of the original brass.

Libraries and book stores have interesting books regarding gravestone and brass rubbings.

Bibliography

JACOBS, G. WALKER. *Stranger Stop and Cast an Eye: A Guide to Gravestones and Gravestone Rubbing.* Brattleboro: Stephen Greene Press, 1973.

ANDREW, LAYE. *Creative Rubbings.* New York: Watson-Guptill Publications, 1968.

BROCKMAN, C. FRANK, and MERILEES, REBECCA. *Trees of North America.* Edited by Herbert S. Zim. New York: Golden Press, 1968.

PETRIDES, GEORGE A. *A Field Guide to Trees and Shrubs.* Boston: Houghton Mifflin, 1958.

NEWCOMB, LAWRENCE. *Newcomb's Wildflower Guide.* Boston: Little Brown, 1977.

PETERSON, ROGER TORY, and MCKENNY, MARGARET. *A Field Guide to Wildflowers.* Boston: Houghton Mifflin, 1968.

COBB, BOUGHTON. *A Field Guide to the Ferns.* Boston: Houghton Mifflin, 1956.

FOSTER, F. GORDON. *The Gardener's Fern Book.* Princeton: Van Nostrand, 1964.

Index

Bark rubbings, 45-7
    paper for, 47
Book covers (decorated
    with leaf rubbings),
    41
Brass rubbing. *See*
    Gravestone rubbing
Children, 18, 40, 49
Crayon
    best kinds, 7-8
    use of, 4, 10
Desk accessories (deco-
    rated with leaf
    rubbings), 44 (*ill.*)
Evergreens, 29-31
Ferns, 26-8
Flower pots (decorated
    with leaf rubbings),
    43
Gift wrappings (using leaf
    rubbings), 40
Grasses, 26-8
Gravestone rubbing, 7,
    52-4

Krylon, 44
Lampshades (decorated
    with leaf rubbings),
    42
Leaf rubbing
    collections of, 18-23
    display of, 16-17, 32-44
    how to make, 3-4 (*ill.*),
        8, 10-11
    versatility as hobby, 1-2
Leaves
    best kinds for rubbing,
        12-13
    identification of, 23-6
    structure of, 24-6 (*ill.*
        25, 26)
Oldstone Enterprises, 8
Paper
    best kinds, 5
    shelf paper, 5, 36
Rubbing crayons. *See
    under* Crayon
Rubbing paper. *See under*
    Paper